The Completely Useless Guide to England

Martin Pullen

COMPLETELY USELESS GUIDES

Also by Martin Pullen

The Completely Useless Guide to London
The Completely Useless Guide to Christmas

A Leisurely Guide to the South West Coast Path
(Minehead to Westward Ho!)

Text and illustrations copyright © Martin Pullen 2019

Martin Pullen has asserted his rights under the Copyright, Designs and Patents Act, 1988, to be identified as the author of this work.

All rights reserved. No part of this publication may be reproduced, stored in a retrieval system or transmitted, in any form or by any means, electronic, mechanical, photocopying, recording or otherwise, without the prior permission of the publisher and copyright holder.

A FETE WORSE THAN DEATH
1 Put Your Left Leg In 7
2 Tom Pearce, Tom Pearce 17
3 Parish News 27
4 Remember, Remember 47

GAME, SET AND MATCH
5 Not-so-Olympic Games 53
6 We Are the Champions 71
7 David Peckham! David Peckham! 86

FOREVER ENGLAND
8 Painting the Town Red 105
9 The Name's Pond ... Duck Pond 111
10 Oh! I do Like to be Beside the Seaside 123
11 Nudge, Nudge, Wink, Wink 133
12 Follywood 138
13 Foreign Correspondence 148
14 Flotsam and Jetsam 155

Capital Letters

This may be a useless guide to England, but it is an even more useless guide to London by way of the fact that the country's capital city does not get a mention. This lack of capital words, or even letters, has occurred due to the previous publication of *The Completely Useless Guide to London*, available now online and one or two bookshops.

A Fete Worse Than Death

Chapter 1

Put Your Left Leg In

*Your left leg out.
In out, in out,
Shake it all about...*

When the Hunchback of Notre Dame exclaimed "The bells, the bells!" he could well have been referring to an approaching troupe of Morris dancers. An English tradition almost as old as the Black Death, troupes of up to eight dancers, dressed most often in white with bell pads on their shins, shake and bang sticks together whilst waving handkerchiefs and jigging about. Members of the troupe (especially the men) often sport bushy, unkempt beards.

Abbots Bromley Horn Dance

Known locally as Wakes Monday, on the first Monday after 5 September in the Staffordshire village of Abbots Bromley, twelve male dancers, including three carrying a set of brown reindeer antler horns and three carrying a set of white, perform the *Abbots Bromley Horn Dance*. Accompanying the dancers – all members of the local Fowell family – is a court jester, a hobbyhorse, a man dressed as Maid Marian and an accordion player, along with two youths, one holding a bow and arrow, the other a triangle.

Following an early morning blessing at St Nicholas Church, where the antlers are kept on display throughout the year, the dancers, dressed in either pink or green waistcoats, knee-length grey trousers, long green socks and faded orange hats somewhat resembling whoopee cushions, set off from the village green to make their way via local farms to Blithfield Hall country house.

In the early afternoon, the dancers retrace their steps, performing outside the village's five pubs and several houses before returning the horns to the church.

Although the first mention of the dance was not until 1686 in Robert Plot's *Natural History of Staffordshire*, the horns themselves have been carbon dated to around 1065.

The Nutters' Dance
Once a year on the morning of Easter Saturday, the streets of the Lancastrian town of Bacup host what has been described as "the most unusual dance in England".

Accompanied by the Stacksteads Brass Band, the Britannia Coconut Dancers – an eight-man clog dancing troupe led by the whip-cracking 'whiffler' – set off from outside the former Travellers Rest pub, wagging fingers, stamping, shaking, tapping, weaving and circling their way through the town.

Together with blackened faces, the troupe sport white turbans, each trimmed with a rosette, blue feather and red pom-pom, black polo-neck sweaters, red and white hooped skirts, white leggings under black knee breeches, a white sash and black clogs.

The troupe's name comes from the maple-wood discs, referred to as nuts, attached to their knees, waists and wrists. When tapped together the nuts act like castanets.

The story tells that the dance along with the clothes and blackened faces, originated from North African Moorish pirates who long ago settled in Cornwall and found work down the local tin mines. In the 18th and

19th centuries, descendants of the pirates moved to the Lancashire coal mines, taking the dance with them. The maple-wood nuts are said to resemble the knee and elbow protection once worn by miners when crawling through narrow seams, and the tapping being the messages miners sent along water pipes when listening out for others trapped following a rock fall.

Filly Loo

Before pipes pumped water to the Dorset village of Ashmore, villagers had to rely on water from the local pond. By custom, in the years when the pond ran dry the villagers would gather in and around the edges of the dried-up bed and hold a feast.

Farmers meanwhile would take the opportunity to dredge the pond of mud, spreading the rich soil on their fields.

Reviving the custom in 1956 (apart from the dry pond, feast and dredging), on the Friday nearest to 24 June, folk dance clubs from Ashmore and surrounding villages gather, along with Morris dancers, for *Filly Loo*. Sounding not unlike a modern invention you put in your toilet cistern to reduce water usage, Filly Loo is a celebration marking Midsummer's Day. The first Filly Loo dance is led by a man dressed in something akin to a compost heap, with celebrations reaching their climax with a local interpretation of the Abbots Bromley Horn Dance, with Maid Marian, court jester, hobbyhorse et al. The evening ends with dancing hand-in-hand around the village pond.

Furry Dance

Legend tells that the Devil was flying over Cornwall, planning to block the entrance to Hell with a massive boulder. St Michael spotted the Devil through the night-time sky and a fight ensued.

The Devil dropped the boulder, and the spot where it landed became known as *Hell's Stone*. Over time, Hell's Stone grew into a small market town, the town of Helston.

An alternative story tells that a great fiery dragon fell to earth, landing in what is now Angel Yard.

For those who doubt either story, embedded in the west wall of the Angel Hotel in Angel Yard is a large chunk of rock, said to be all that remains of whatever it was that fell to earth that day.

Ignoring the likelihood of it being a meteorite, locals, happy that either St Michael defeated the Devil or that their town survived the impact of a great fiery dragon falling to earth, celebrated – and continue to celebrate each year on *Helston Flora Day* – by performing the *Furry Dance*. The dance is thought to date back to pre-Christian times, the name probably coming from *feur*, the Celtic word for festival. Also known as *The Flora*, with lyrics added by a Katie Moss in 1911, the song has since been recorded several times, perhaps most notably by Terry Wogan as *The Floral Dance*.

Marking the passing of winter and the arrival of summer, Helston Flora Day is celebrated on 8 May (or the previous Saturday if 8 May falls on a Sunday or Monday). The day begins with the *Servants of the Gentry Dance*, followed by *Hal-an-Tal*, a lively dance-cum-mummers' mystery play. The play is not so much of a mystery as it involves Robin Hood, Friar Tuck, St Michael and St George, with St George slaying a dragon in a battle of good against evil.

As the play unfolds, performers sing *Hal-an-Tal*...

What happened to the Spaniard
That made so brave a boast-O
That they would eat the feathered goose
And we would eat the roast-O

...the tale of the Spanish raid on Newlyn in 1595 at the start of the Anglo-Spanish war, when 400 men under the command of Carlos de Amésquita attacked the town, apparently in search of a goose lunch.

Following the Children's Dance, midday sees the *Dance of the Gentry*, with men in formal wear and ladies with flowing ball gowns and flowery hats. Whilst led by the

Helston Brass Band with their rendition of *The Floral Dance*, the Gentry dance through gardens, shops and local houses, welcoming the onset of the warmth of summer.

Chapter 2

Tom Pearce, Tom Pearce, Lend Me Your Grey Mare

All along, down along, out along, lee
For I want to go to Widecombe Fair
Wi' Bill Brewer, Jan Stewer, Peter Gurney,
Peter Davy, Dan'l Whiddon, Harry Hawke,
Old Uncle Tom Cobley and all,
Old Uncle Tom Cobley and all.

From Bill Brewer to Old Uncle Tom Cobley, if there is one thing the English enjoy more than queuing or talking about the weather, it's a fete, fair or festival. Especially if it is raining and there's a queue for the portable toilets...

Rochester Sweeps Festival

Held over the May Day weekend in the Kent town of Rochester, the *Rochester Sweeps Festival* celebrates what was traditionally the first time off for chimney sweeps following the busy winter months.

Festivities begin at dawn on Blue Bell Hill with a ceremonial awakening of Jack-in-the-Green, a pagan symbol of fertility, featuring a tall man disguised as a section of privet hedge.

Along with chimney sweeps and folk dancers, over 60 Morris dancing troupes then gather in the grounds of Rochester Castle for a procession through the town's streets.

Slaithwaite Moonraking Festival

Every other February in odd-numbered years during the week of the Kirklees Schools' half term holiday, the West Yorkshire village of Slaithwaite celebrates with a Moonraking Festival. Billed as a week of lantern making and storytelling, and what better story to tell than that of the moon-raking smugglers...

The year was 1802. The Huddersfield Narrow Canal, so named due to its lack of width, had recently opened. Running through the middle of the village, the canal soon became a busy trade route; it also enjoyed a side-line in the smuggling of rum and whisky. One day, as the smugglers were going about their dodgy dealings, they spotted a Customs and Excise officer approaching. Quick thinking, they offloaded their barrels of illicit alcohol into the reeds at the side of the canal.

Later the smugglers returned to retrieve their contraband, dragging the barrels from the reeds with large garden rakes. This time, two Customs and Excise officers approached and, failing to spot the barrels, enquired as to what the men were doing on such a cold moonlit February evening. With the moon reflected in the water of the canal, one of the quick-thinking smugglers explained in a drunken voice that the moon had fallen into the canal and that they were having to rake it out.

The officers laughed, calling them silly moonrakers, and went on their way.

The *Slaithwaite Moonraking Festival* commemorates the legend of the cunning smugglers, whose sharp-wittedness fooled the Customs and Excise officers. The highlight of the festival is on the evening of the second Saturday of the school holiday when a giant illuminated crescent Moon is floated down the canal on a barge.

Moon Maidens first rake the Moon from the canal and then Gnomes parade the Moon around the village, leading a spectacular procession with over 200 illuminated paper and willow lanterns in the shape of everything from animals to stars, rockets and planets.

Followed by several thousand locals, the parade ends back at the canal with fire-eaters, street entertainers, music and a firework display.

Hungerford Hocktide Festival
Way back in the 14th century, John of Gaunt, 1st Duke of Lancaster, granted special fishing and grazing rights to

the common people of the Berkshire town of Hungerford. Around 100 properties still hold these commoners' rights, and on the Friday following Easter Sunday the properties' owners meet to form a special Hocktide Council. The council duly appoints a Constable and two Tutti-Men.

On the following Hock Tuesday – known locally as Tutti-Day – the Tutti-Men, each carrying a clove-studded orange atop a decorative Tutti-Pole, call on the commoners' houses. Accompanied by the Orange-Man (wearing a feather-decorated hat and carrying a sack of oranges) the Tutti-Men exchange oranges for either a financial donation or kiss from the head of the house.

Meanwhile, Tutti-Wenches, also in exchange for money or kisses, give out oranges to the accompanying crowd.

The commoners then attend a special Hocktide Lunch, followed by an initiation ceremony for all first-time attendees. Known as *Shoeing the Colts*, the attendees' legs are held whilst the local blacksmith hammers a nail into one of their shoes.

The day ends with the tossing of oranges and heated coins to the gathered children from the steps of the Town Hall.

Thought to have originated from a nosegay, the clove and flowery aroma of the Tutti Poles was once said to alleviate (with no disrespect to the commoners of Hungerford) the smell from some of the less wholesome parts of town.

Whittlesea Straw Bear Festival

On the second or third Saturday in January, a man dressed in what one would loosely describe as a bear costume made from straw is paraded through the streets of the Cambridgeshire town of Whittlesey, escorted by a man sporting a red cravat and bowler hat, carrying a cane and with string tied around his waist and knees.

The straw bear man is followed by a procession of costumed characters, including a reindeer and giant chicken.

Adding to the excitement are a drummer, an accordion player and various other musicians, together with over 250 Molly, Morris, clog and sword dancers.

The following day, the adult bear – hopefully without the costume's occupant – is burned. The custom, a celebration of the wheat harvest, is thought to date back to the 19th century. And if you think you've spotted a typographical error, despite its name change Whittlesey still retains the earlier spelling of Whittlesea for both its train station and *Straw Bear Festival*.

Banbury Hobby Horse Festival
Ride a cockhorse to Banbury Cross
To see a fine lady upon a white horse
With rings on her fingers and bells on her toes
She shall have music wherever she goes.

The second weekend of October sees the Oxfordshire town of Banbury host the annual hobbyhorse festival, with a parade, racing and Morris dancing.

A prize is awarded for the best fancy dress, which, as one might expect, is a hobbyhorse costume.

Nottingham Goose Fair
Dating back to the late 13th century, Nottingham Goose Fair was so named as each year up to 20,000 geese were driven from the Lincolnshire Fens to be sold at the eight-day event.

Alongside the geese, the fair was also renowned for the sale of anything from animal livestock to women.

Later gaining a reputation for its high quality cheese, in 1764 a one-third jump in prices resulted in a riot, with huge cheeses rolled down the streets and – following the local mayor being bowled over by a large truckle of cheese – mounted guards sent in to quell the angry mob.

With cheese, geese and wife sales having given way to funfair rides, Nottingham Goose Fair – now reduced to five days – is held annually at the start of October.

Chapter 3

Parish News

Before detailed maps of the English countryside were drawn up marking parish boundaries, on Ascension Day, 40 days after Easter Sunday, villagers led by the local priest, church officials and choirboys, would walk the lanes and fields of their parish checking on the location of the boundary stones. The stones were important as they were a way of checking that land had not been encroached upon by a neighbouring parish. It was important to know that the parish boundaries had not moved as taxes levied upon landowners helped maintain the church and local services and determined who had the right of burial within the church grounds.

Upon reaching a boundary stone the choirboys were, if lucky, called upon to beat the 'bound' with a stripped willow branch. If unlucky, they were held upside down by their ankles and their head bumped against the stone – a ritual thought to guarantee that the suffering child would not forget the location of the stone, thereby ensuring that such information was passed down through subsequent generations. To this

day, minus the head banging, many parishes still maintain the ancient beating the bounds custom.

Dating to the 11th century, the Parish Church of St Michael at the North Gate's location in Cornmarket Street – now a busy shopping thoroughfare in the heart of Oxford – makes the annual Ascension Day event somewhat more challenging than when Oxford was once a walled city. Of the 31 remaining boundary markers, many are now incorporated within commercial buildings and shops, including a storage area under the Covered Market…

...and a metal cross on the floor of Wagamama's noodle bar.

Whilst another boundary stone is preserved in a glass cabinet mounted on the wall in Marks and Spencer's department store, a metal cross marking the true boundary location is set into the floor of the women's underwear department, reputedly hidden at times under a rack of bras. Shoppers are somewhat taken aback to observe the local vicar chalking the words 'St Michael of the North Gate' along with the year on the cross as the city mayor, college lecturers, choristers and various entourage chant 'Mark! Mark! Mark!' and proceed to whip the floor with stripped willow branches. One can only imagine the resultant queue at customer enquiries.

The final 'bound' is in the courtyard of Lincoln College, where students toss pennies from the tower to schoolchildren below. The pennies are heated as a warning of the sin of avarice.

Following the beating of the bounds, the college treats the vicar and his entourage to a hearty meal of ploughman's lunch and doughnuts washed down with a glass of beer. Served only on Ascension Day, the beer, made from ground ivy, is brewed to a secret recipe said to have at one time been known only by Alf the kitchen man.

Weighing the Mayor
Legend tells that, upon a visit to the Buckinghamshire town of High Wycombe, Queen Elizabeth I commented on the robust proportions of the mayor and members of his elected office. With the queen inferring that the portly mayor and other town officials may have spent their time in office dining lavishly at taxpayers' expense, the tradition arose whereby upon entering and later retiring from office the mayor would be weighed. Consequently, on the third Saturday in May a large weighing seat is placed in the centre of High Wycombe, upon which the newly elected mayor together with the retiring mayor is submitted to the public humiliation.

And, just to make sure that the public purse is not being squandered on lavish meals, the aldermen, town councillors, honorary freemen and burgesses, charter trustees and anyone else in a position to gain weight at the taxpayers' expense, also submit to the scales.

As the Inspector of Weights and Measures notes each official's weight, the Macebearer declares the result to the gathered crowd. If the outgoing mayor or any member of the elected council has put on weight during their time in office, the Macebearer first states their original weight then declares "and some more", upon which the crowd boo and jeer. If weight has been lost, the Macebearer declares "and no more", a result met with applause.

Luckily for the mayor and accompanying officials, some traditions have been lost to time, as in the past a result of "and some more" would have been met with a barrage of tomatoes and rotten fruit.

Swan Upping
The third week in July marks the start of Swan Upping, an annual census in which mute swans on the River Thames, having been rounded up, counted and given a quick health check, are then released.

A lucky escape for the swans, for in the 12th century they were rounded up and eaten by members of the royal family, the monarchy claiming ownership of all Thames' swans in order to ensure an ample supply for the royal meal table.

Since a 15th-century Royal Charter, co-ownership of the Thames' mute swans has been between the monarchy and two Livery Companies of the City of London: The *Worshipful Company of Vintners* and the *Worshipful Company of Dyers*. During the five-day ceremony, Swan Uppers dressed in scarlet uniforms with matching flat caps row up the Thames in skiffs from Sunbury to Abingdon. Swans caught by the Queen's Swan Uppers are marked with a single ring that links to the British Trust for Ornithology database. Further rings mark the remaining swans depending on whether caught by the Vintners or Dyers.

Oak Apple Day
Formerly a public holiday in England, May 29, *Oak Apple Day*, commemorated the Restoration of the monarchy with the crowning of King Charles II in 1660. The name refers to Charles seeking refuge in an oak tree following his defeat at the Battle of Worcester, marking the end of the English Civil War.

Oak Apple Day in the Wiltshire village of Great Wishford is an altogether different affair, being an annual reassertion of 12th-century rights to collect oak tree boughs for use as firewood from nearby Grovely Woods, owned by the Earl of Pembroke. Since incorporated into a charter in 1603, many court battles were fought to retain the ancient rights, with agreement only finally being reached in 1987.

The day begins early with villagers awoken by the sounds of the Rough Band (a group of musicians possibly less welcome than a pork spit roast at a bar mitzvah) banging dustbin lids, ringing bells and blowing trumpets whilst chanting "Grovely! Grovely! Grovely! And all Grovely!"

The not-so-melodic awakening is followed by a procession into Grovely Woods to gather boughs of oak. The best – deemed the Marriage Bough – is hung from the tower of St Giles' Church, where it is said to bring good luck to all couples marrying in the church thereafter.

Villagers then display the remaining boughs outside their houses for later judgment in the Best Bough competition. The winner is the bough that most resembles the antlers of a deer and, importantly, contains oak apples.

Unlikely to be stocked at your local greengrocers, oak apples are abnormal oak tree growths caused by parasites, insects, mites, bacteria and fungi. About the size of golf balls and marginally less appetizing, they originate from chemicals released from the hatching eggs of female gall wasps.

Under the terms of the 1603 charter villagers must then proclaim their bough-collecting rights outside Salisbury Cathedral. Following the declaration once again of "Grovely! Grovely! Grovely! And all Grovely!"

four Nitch Ladies perform a traditional dance on the steps of the cathedral's north porch. Dressed in black skirts and white blouses covered with beige aprons, the bonneted women, each carrying a symbolic bundle of wood known as a 'nitch', are a tribute to Grace Reed, imprisoned in 1825 for attempting to gather firewood in Grovely Woods.

The Oak Apple Day reassertion of rights concludes with the laying of an oak bough at the cathedral altar, then all return to the village for a jolly good knees-up. Cue the Morris dancers...

Old Man's Day
The date was 2 October 1571 and a funeral service for Mathew Wall was about to get underway at St Mary's Church in the Hertfordshire village of Braughing.

Unfortunately, as pallbearers carried the coffin along the tree-lined Fleece Lane, one of the men lost his footing on the slimy autumn leaves and Wall's coffin fell to the ground. Suddenly from within a frantic knocking sound was heard; the young farmer, who had died unexpectedly, had been jolted back to life.

Marrying soon after, Mathew Wall went on to live for another 24 years. Upon his death his will stipulated that each year on *Old Man's Day* – the anniversary of his fortuitous escape – a poor man should be paid to sweep Fleece Lane clear of leaves. The £1 payment was to come from a bequest that he left to the village, along with a further £1 payable by whoever was now living in Quilters, the house and piece of land that he owned in the village.

He also asked for his grave to be planted with brambles to discourage the grazing of sheep, and that the church bell should first ring a funeral toll and then, following a short service at his grave, a wedding peal in celebration of his marriage soon after his unexpected return to life.

Diverting money from the poor, the annual Old Man's Day sweeping of Fleece Lane is now conducted by the church vicar aided by local schoolchildren, with the £2 payment going into the collection box.

The Hunting of the Earl of Rone

Friday of Spring Bank Holiday weekend sees the locals of the Devon village and parish of Combe Martin begin the annual celebration of *The Hunting of the Earl of Rone*. The weekend kicks off with the 'Earl', disguised in a suit of straw-stuffed sacking with wooden 'ship's biscuits' hung from his neck and face hidden behind a red, white and blue mask, attempting to evade capture from a band of fake Grenadier Guards.

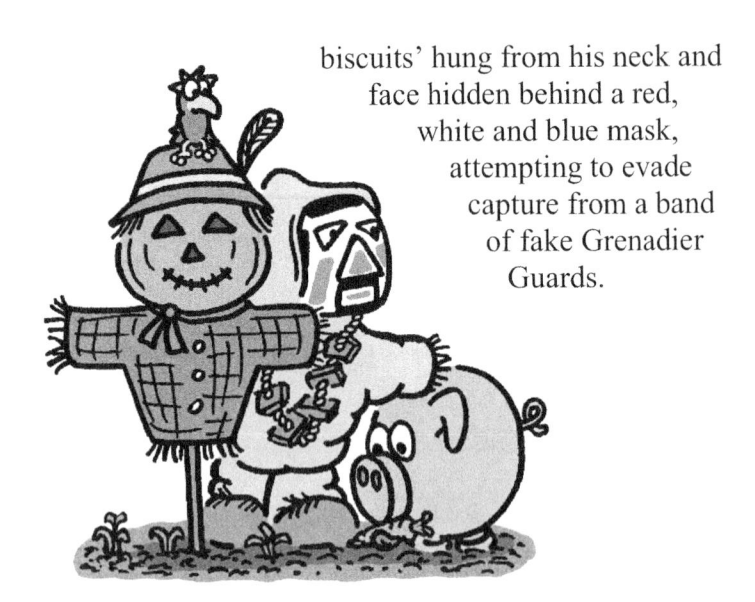

Dressed in red tunics with black breeches, the guards sport colourful pointy hats that appear to be made from the remnants of children's Christmas paper chain decorations.

The fake Grenadiers are aided in their search by massed parishioners, the women dressed in 19th-century 'peasant' costume, the men dressed in breeches and smocks, with top hats, bowlers or flat caps. Bloodhounds they are not, as it is not until the Monday evening when two drummers lead the baying pack up to Lady Wood, that the Earl, cornered hiding amongst the trees, is finally arrested.

Dutifully seated backwards on a donkey, the Earl is paraded through the main street of the village, pausing to be 'shot' at intervals by his guards.

Falling dead to the floor, following revival by the 'Fool', he is helped back onto the donkey by a hobbyhorse, the horse inexplicably masquerading as a giant fairy cake.

Upon reaching the beach, the Earl receives a final bullet and falls to the sand, dead. The crowd cheers as the Grenadiers then wade into the water, tossing an effigy of the Earl out to sea.

Legend tells that The Hunting of the Earl of Rone dates to Sir Hugh O'Neill, the Earl of Tyrone, who opposed English rule in Ireland. Following defeat in the Nine Years' War, in 1607 the earl fled his native Ireland, his journey ending shipwrecked on the North Devon coast in Rapparee Cove, west of Combe Martin. Surviving only on ship's biscuits, O'Neill hid from search parties in Lady Wood until captured by Grenadier Guards.

Truth be known, fearing their enemies were plotting their execution O'Neill along with a group of fellow Irish chieftains sailed to the safety of Spain. With the earl failing to set foot on English soil, exactly why the villagers of Combe Martin celebrate the ancient tradition of Hunting the Earl of Rone has been lost to the misty seas of time.

The Dunmow Flitch Trials
The story goes that, concealing their identities, the Lord of the Manor and his good Lady wife asked the prior of Little Dunmow Priory to bless their happy marriage of a year and a day. The prior, warmed by the couple's love and dedication, rewarded them with a flitch, otherwise known as a side of bacon.

Revealing his identity, the lord donated land to the Priory upon the condition that henceforth couples who could prove similar allegiance would also receive a flitch. However, proof was not to be easily gained as it would mean undergoing a trial by marital-jury – a *Dunmow Flitch Trial*.

First held in the Essex village of Little Dunmow, the Dunmow Flitch Trials are thought to date back as far as 1104. Revived following the Second World War, the modern trials are held just once every four years, in July of a leap year in the neighbouring town of Great Dunmow.

The day begins with the town crier leading a procession of officials to a marquee, where the mock court is to sit. In sessions throughout the day five couples take their turn to convince the presiding judge that in 'twelvemonth and a day' they have 'not wisht themselves unmarried again'. Whilst a clerk of the court takes notes and an usher ensures order in the public gallery, a jury of six bachelors and six maidens listen as the prosecution and defence councils – often barristers in real life – argue their case.

As day turns to evening, a procession sets off for the marquee courtroom headed by 'eight humble peasant folk', who parade the Flitch in a wooden frame decorated with ribbons and foliage. Close behind, further humble folk carry both the ancient wooden Flitch Chair and a not so ancient but much less likely to fall apart when sat upon, new Flitch Chair.

Couples who have successfully proven their allegiance and won their flitch are carried on the not so ancient Flitch Chair to Market Place, where they kneel on pointed stones to swear the Flitch Oath.

You do swear by custom of confession
That you ne'er made nuptial transgression
Nor since you were married man and wife
By household brawls or contentious strife
Or otherwise in bed or at board
Offended each other in deed or in word...

Couples who fail to prove their love and dedication still leave the court with a small joint of gammon, although in shame they must walk through the streets behind the empty Flitch Chair.

Turning the Devil's Stone
At eight o'clock on the evening of 5 November, a cacophony sounds throughout the Devon village of Shebbear as bellringers ring out a jarring peal from the tower of St Michael's Church.

With the Devil hopefully kept at bay by the tuneless tune, the discordant campanologists exit the church, crowbars in hand, and make their way to the nearby village green, where under an ancient oak tree sits what is known locally as the Devil's Stone. As the vicar recites a prayer, the bellringers surround the stone and shouting excitedly, turn it over.

Local legend tells that the stone fell from the Devil's pocket as he fought with God and he was trapped beneath it. Turning the stone ensures that his efforts to tunnel free remain fruitless. If the stone were not to be turned a disaster would befall the village.

On more solid ground, geology suggests that the misplaced stone may have been deposited at the end of the last ice age; otherwise it could be the remnant of a standing stone or an altar stone dating back to pagan times.

As the expression goes, never let the truth get in the way of a good story, and – returning to legend – a further story goes that the stone was quarried locally for use as the foundation stone for Henscott Church, to be built on the other side of the River Torridge at nearby Bradford, but the Devil kept bringing it back to Shebbear.

Eventually, the builders gave up and left it there. Either way, with the stone turned for another year, villagers retire to the nearby Devil's Stone Inn for liquid refreshment.

Chapter 4

Remember, Remember, the Fifth of November

*Gunpowder, treason and plot
I see no reason why gunpowder treason
Should ever be forgot.*

Turning the Devil's Stone is not the only thing that happens on 5 November. In the late 15th and early 16th century England was strongly protestant. Catholics, suppressed in their faith, were treated with suspicion as potential traitors. And traitors they proved to be, when several rebellious Catholics plotted to kill King James I by blowing up the chamber of the House of Lords on 5 November 1605, the day of the Annual State Opening of Parliament. Following a tip-off, the evening before the king was due to arrive guards searched the cellars below the House of Lords. With matches and fuses in pocket, the rebels' leader Guido 'Guy' Fawkes was found with 36 barrels of gunpowder.

Convicted of treason, in January 1606 Fawkes and seven of his co-conspirators were hanged, drawn and quartered in Westminster's Old Palace Yard. A Parliamentary Act was subsequently passed declaring 5 November a day of thanksgiving for 'the joyful day of deliverance', the day to be marked with bellringing and bonfires.

Although the Act was repealed in 1859, the celebrations, unlike Guy Fawkes himself, live on…

Lewes Bonfire Night
At the time of the Marian Persecutions of 1555-1557, seventeen Protestant religious reformers were burned at the stake in front of what is now Lewes Town Hall. Marking both the uncovering of the Gunpowder Plot and the execution of the seventeen Protestant martyrs, on 5 November seventeen burning crosses along with effigies of Guy Fawkes, Camillo Borghese – Pope at the time of the infamous plot – and other currently derided public figures, are paraded through the East Sussex town.

Accompanying the parade are upwards of 3,000 marchers dressed in traditional smugglers' uniform of striped jumper, white trousers, black boots and red hat, each holding aloft flaming torches. (Exactly why smugglers, not wishing to be seen carrying their ill-gotten booty, wore striped jumpers, white trousers, black boots and red hats is best left for another time.)

Amidst the smoke and flames, the non-inconspicuous smugglers toss 'bangers' to the floor, exploding close to the feet of the gathered crowd.

The evening begins with a barrel of burning tar, thrown into the River Ouse to mark the tossing of local magistrates into the river in 1847 following their reading of the Riot Act to what was known as the 'bonfire boys'.

Following the parade, the evening ends with five separate bonfire and firework displays, where the effigies meet an ignoble end.

Ottery St Mary Tar Barrels
Wearing no more protection than oversized oven gloves, residents of the Devon town of Ottery St Mary celebrate Guy Fawkes Night by running a relay through the streets, each carrying aloft one of seventeen flaming wooden barrels. The barrels are first lined with coal tar and stuffed with paper and

straw, the highly inflammable contents then soaked in paraffin before the open end of the barrel is set alight.

It sounds so inviting I would love to take part myself, were it not for my fear of oversized oven gloves.

Game, Set and Match

Chapter 5

Not-so-Olympic Games

First held in 1612, exactly 400 years before the London 2012 Olympics, the *Cotswold Olimpicks* were described by the British Olympic Association as 'the first stirrings of Britain's Olympic beginnings.' First stirrings they were as, long before the coming of synchronised swimming and beach volleyball, original Olimpick events included sledgehammer tossing, pike-drill and shin-kicking, a sport whereby men dressed in white shepherd's smocks would attempt to kick each other's shins.

Unlike the modern sack race, popular at school sports day, the Olimpicks' sack race saw the sack tied at the competitor's neck, restricting use of their arms for balance.

The sports were played out in front of a makeshift wooden castle, with a small cannon fired to signal the start of each event.

The events were refereed by 'sticklers', so called as they used long sticks to separate battling swordsmen. From sticklers we gain the English expression 'a stickler for the rules.'

Held on the Friday following the Spring Bank Holiday close to the Gloucestershire town of Chipping Campden, the Cotswold Olimpicks are contested on what is now Dover's Hill, the hill named in honour of the Olimpicks' founder, a local lawyer by the name of Robert Dover. Although still no beach volleyball, modern events include piano-smashing, gurning and dwile-flonking. Speaking of which...

Dwile Flonking
With dwile coming from the Dutch word for mop and flonk derived from flong, the former past tense of fling, the rules of dwile flonking centre around a bucket (or often a chamber pot) of beer and the flinging of a knitted floor cloth. The game involves two teams of between eight and ten players, dressed in authentic 'country' costume of floppy hat, baggy white shirt under a waistcoat, and trousers secured with binder twine at the knee. Following the appointment of a 'dull-witted

person' as referee, the toss of a sugar beet determines the team to go first. The referee shouts "Here y'go t'gither", and the game begins. Members of the non-flonking team then lock hands and perform a skip-like dance known as a girt, whilst circling the flonking teams elected flonker. As they do so the flonker dunks his dwile-tipped driveller – a stick made from the wood of a hazel or yew tree – into the pot of beer and circling in the opposite direction to the girters attempts to flonk them with his dwile.

If the dwile misses the girters form a line and chant "pot, pot, pot" as they pass the wet dwile from hand to hand. Before the dwile reaches the end of the line, the flonker must down the contents of the pot. The contents of the pot used to be by tradition beer but with modern Health and Safety laws forbidding games that involve the speedy-consumption of alcohol, a recent rule change now allows the girter to pour the contents over his head.

The game consists of four snurds, with points awarded for wantons, morthers and ripples. All quite simple really.

Dwile flonking is played at several pubs in Suffolk and – as *dwyle flunking* – at the Lewes Arms, in the East Sussex town of Lewes.

Wenlock Olympian Games
After reading of the premature deaths of non-exercising weavers, in 1850 a Dr William Penny Brookes established the *Wenlock Olympian Games* in the Shropshire town of Much Wenlock. Considered the forerunner of the modern Olympics, original events

included athletics, football and cycling, albeit the cycling on penny-farthings...

...whilst sadly overlooked in modern Olympic schedules, other fun events included the Old Women's Race and blindfolded wheelbarrow racing.

Following the Games' success, Brookes went on to cofound the National Olympic Association, with the first National Olympic Games held in 1866 in London. And in recognition of the Wenlock Olympian Games, still held annually in July, one of the two mascots for the London 2012 Summer Olympics was named Wenlock.

International Bognor Birdman
According to the popular quote, if God had meant us to fly, he would have given us wings. He didn't but that hasn't stopped us trying, particularly in the seaside resort of Bognor Regis, where over a summer weekend, entrants attempt to recreate the flight of a bird by launching themselves from the end of the pier, with the coveted Birdman Trophy awarded to the 'human-powered flying machine' who glides the furthest distance. Aside from wings and feathers, the wearing of costumes is encouraged, with previous entrants having included a sugar plum fairy…

...a waddle of penguins...

...and a skateboarding cow.

In 2009, gliding the furthest distance proved impossible as, following storm damage the previous year, eighteen metres of the pier had to be removed. Whilst repairs were being undertaken the competition was moved to nearby Worthing, which now continues with its own Birdman weekend.

The Great Knaresborough Bed Race
The month of June in the historic North Yorkshire market town of Knaresborough sees around 25,000 spectators and 90 teams gather at the Castle Ground for the start of the annual *Great Bed Race*.

Following a parade of marching bands, dance troupes and the awarding of trophies for the best-dressed bed and most entertaining team, competitors remove the elaborate decorations and prepare to set off on a course through the town's streets.

Each team consists of six bed-pushers, with a further bed-ridden passenger wearing precautionary helmet and lifejacket, considered necessary as towards the end of the race the teams wade across the River Nidd.

Cooper's Hill Cheese-Rolling and Wake
Traditionally held on Spring Bank Holiday, *Cooper's Hill Cheese-Rolling and Wake* saw competitors chase a large cylindrical block of Double Gloucester cheese 230 metres down the extremely steep Gloucestershire hill. Given a one-second head start and reaching a speed of over 60 mph, suffice to say, the cheese always evaded capture.

Attracting a crowd four times bigger than can comfortably fit on Cooper's Hill without collectively breathing in and following multiple injuries requiring paramedics and an air ambulance, in 2010 the event was officially cancelled and has remained so ever since.

Nevertheless, the famed Cheese-Rolling and Wake lives on, albeit without the blessing of the local authority.

Cheshire Cheese Rolling Championships

A somewhat more sedate affair, the city of Chester used to host the *Cheshire Cheese Rolling Championships*. In a relay, competing teams would roll a wooden copy of the traditional cheese-wheel down Bridge Street following an obstacle course of hay bales and wooden farmyard animals, before returning up the hill. Sadly, the championships appear to be no more; the city of Chester has moooooved on to other forms of entertainment.

Oxenhope Straw Race

In the mid-1970s, with entertainment not being what it is today, two men in the West Yorkshire village of Oxenhope decided to pass the time by challenging each other to a race between pubs whilst carrying a bale of straw. Becoming an annual event, with two competitors per team July sees around 250 teams quite often in fancy dress attempt to complete a 2.5-mile course through the village carrying a 20-kg bale of straw, pausing only to consume a pint of beer at each of the pubs en route.

Setting off at midday from the Waggon and Horses, competitors, run to the Bale Horse, where they down a pint and pick up their bale of straw.

From there they continue via the Oxenhope Social Club, the Lamb Inn and the Leg of Mutton, finally five pints later crossing the finish line at the Dog and Gun in Denholme Road. Finishing times range from around fifteen minutes to quite simply not finishing.

Crantock Bale Push Championships
Not to be outdone by Oxenhope, on the second Friday in September the Cornish village of Crantock plays host to the *Bale Push Championships*, with teams of four pushing a bale of straw the size of a tractor wheel and width of a car through the village, the start and end lines defined by The Cornishman and Old Albion pubs.

Surfing the Severn Bore
With the tidal level in the Bristol Channel at times rising by over 15 metres, the funnelling of water into the narrowing estuary of the River Severn creates a large surge wave known as the Severn Bore. Popular with surfers, the wave can travel as far as 20 miles upriver.

Llanymynech Rocks Golf

Perched atop sheer cliff faces, Llanymynech Rocks Golf Club has the only 18-hole course that is in both England and Wales. Club members tee-off on the 4th in Wales, putting to the hole in England, before returning to Wales at the 7th tee.

Maldon Mud Race

The Essex town of Maldon resides on the estuary of the River Blackwater. On either the Sunday or Monday of Spring Bank Holiday, whilst the river is at low tide, around 300 competitors mostly in fancy dress attempt to wade through the waist-deep mud of the riverbank, crossing the water to continue through the mud on the far side, before returning. The course covers 400 metres, and as the front-"runners" churn the mud underfoot, becomes somewhat more difficult than snorkelling in custard. Not that I have ever snorkelled in custard.

UK Wife Carrying Race

Wife carrying, legend tells, is a long-established Scandinavian tradition practised in readiness for the stealing of women, married or otherwise from neighbouring villages. Whether the Surrey town of Dorking is preparing itself for such activity is unclear; however, the *UK Wife Carrying Race* is part of the annual calendar on The Nower, a sloping piece of common ground off Hampstead Lane. Held on a Sunday in March, couples compete over a 380-metre course, first prize being a large keg of ale from the local Pilgrim Brewery, with the last placed couple receiving a Pot Noodle and tin of dog food; ironically, Winalot.

A special prize of a string of sausages is awarded to the carrier who completes the course with the heaviest wife, whilst the oldest carrier receives a jar of Bovril and tin of pilchards. Somewhat liberal rules state that 'wives' don't need to be female; they must however weigh at least 50 kgs or make up the deficit by carrying tins of baked beans.

Bramble Bank Cricket Match
Before relaxation of licensing laws, English pubs were limited in their opening hours. None more limited than the Bramble Inn, open for only one hour a year and that dependent on the low spring tide. For the Bramble Inn – little more than a table, parasol and couple of plastic chairs – is set in place to serve the spectators and participants of the Bramble Bank Cricket Match, held on the one occasion each year that The Brambles sandbank briefly emerges from the busy waters of The Solent.

The limited-over match lasts between 30 minutes and an hour, dependent on the length of time that the 200-yard-long sandbank – 1.5 miles out to sea between Southampton and the Isle of Wight – remains above water. As the sandbank emerges, members of the Royal Southern Yacht Club from the mainland village of Hamble-le-Rice disembark and take wicket against members of the Island Sailing Club from Cowes.

The teams dress in traditional cricketing whites for the occasion, and contrary to normal sporting convention the winning side is pre-decided, the clubs taking it in turns to lift the trophy.

Due to currents and tidal flow, each year The Brambles sandbank emerges a little further west, destined at some point to remain forever submerged. Until then, let the game live on.

Chapter 6

We Are the Champions!

When former Queen lead singer Freddie Mercury penned *We Are the Champions*, I don't imagine he was writing of the band's success in any of the following...

World Worm-Charming Championships
The highlight of summer in the Cheshire village of Willaston is without a doubt the *World Worm-Charming Championships*. Competitors, designated a three-metre square plot of earth, have 30 minutes to 'charm' by whatever means possible as many worms to the surface: the most popular technique – known as twanging – being to push a garden fork into the ground and create vibrations by tapping the handle with a stick.

Other worm-charming methods have included the use of cricket stumps and a bat…

…knitting needles…

...and a bottle xylophone.

Long presumed that the vibrations created by the noise fool the inquisitive worms into thinking that it's raining, recent research has revealed that the worms could be confusing the vibrations for a similar sound made by moles, the worm's worst predator. A single mole can eat up to its own weight in worms every day.

At the first World Worm-Charming Championships in 1980, Tom Shufflebotham charmed 511 worms out of his pre-metric three-yard square plot, a record catch that stood until 2009.

With such a count to beat, over the years the championships have been the subject of dirty tricks, with one charmer banned for life after concealing 'spare' worms in his trouser legs, held in place by the wearing of bicycle clips…

…whilst another charmer was caught chopping their worms in half to double their score.

Wriggle out of that one!

Welly-Wanging World Championships

With *wang* being the Yorkshire word for throw, welly-wanging is not dissimilar to the Olympic discus or hammer tossing event, only using a wellington boot. To be precise, a Dunlop green welly size 9.

Held each June as part of the West Yorkshire village of Upperthong's annual Gala Weekend, *Welly-Wanging World Championship* competitors, given a maximum run-up of 42 paces, 'wang' their welly as far as possible, aiming to land within boundary lines defined by the Holme Moss TV mast to one side and Longley Farm windmill to the other.

World Black Pudding Throwing Championships

Nestled in a valley just north of Manchester is the West Pennine Moor town of Ramsbottom. For those who enjoy sports that involve congealed blood, perhaps Ramsbottom's greatest claim to fame is the *World Black Pudding Throwing Championships*, held mid-September outside the Royal Oak Pub on Bridge Street.

Tossing underarm, contestants, armed with a black pudding wrapped in a pair of tights, have three attempts to knock down a twelve-high stack of Yorkshire puddings atop a platform six metres above the ground.

With a not-overly-complicated scoring system, whoever knocks down the most Yorkshire puddings wins.

World Egg-Throwing Championships
In the 14th century, all chickens in the Lincolnshire hamlet of Swaton came under the control of the abbot of the local monastery. To ensure attendance at the local church, parishioners who attended Sunday prayer would receive the gift of an egg. When in 1322 the River Eau flooded and parishioners were unable to get to church, according to legend the new abbot instructed his monks to throw the eggs to them across the swollen river.

In remembrance of the Abbot of Swaton, the annual *World Egg-Throwing Championships*, held on the last Sunday in June as part of Swaton Vintage Day, has grown from its inauguration in 2005 to encompass such events as Russian Egg Roulette and the Egg Trebuchet Challenge. Much eggcitement to be had!

World Gravy Wrestling Championships
If you are looking for something a little saucy, the *World Gravy Wrestling Championships* are held on August Bank Holiday Monday outside the Rose 'n' Bowl pub in the Lancashire village of Stacksteads. In separate events, men and women compete in a knockout competition, each wrestling match contested in a paddling pool of gravy lasting two minutes. Points are awarded more for the quality of fancy dress than wrestling ability.

World Conker Championships
On the second Sunday in October the Northamptonshire village of Southwick plays host to the *World Conker Championships*. Armed with only a horse chestnut and a twelve-inch shoelace, entrants attempt to smash each other's nuts for the honoured title of King or Queen Conker. The championships – first held in 1965 on the village green in nearby Ashton – came about as alternative entertainment following the abandoning by local pub regulars of a planned fishing trip due to bad weather.

Traditionally a children's game, the earliest recorded reference to the playing of conkers was in 1848 on the Isle of Wight. The game evolved from a similar game, played in the 15th century using snail shells.

World Pie-Eating Championships
The expression 'to eat humble pie' dates to the 1926 General Strike, when miners in the Lancastrian town of Wigan were starved back to work. Those who remained out of work could barely afford to eat humble pie: the intestines and other less savoury innards of deer. In celebration of Wigan's pie-eating past the town is home to the *World Pie Eating Championships*, held mid-December at Harry's Bar on Wallgate.

The championships hit the headlines in 2013 when following Health and Safety concerns it went topless. What you may ask prompted the wanton exposure of bare flesh: with it feared that retained heat could cause burning to the upper mouth, the competition pies were served without crusts.

World Stinging Nettle Eating Championships
Following a dispute in 1986 between two farmers as to whose field contained the longest stinging nettles, one of the farmers, Alex Williams, declared that he would eat any nettle found to be longer than one from his own field. Stemming from these humble roots, the *World Stinging Nettle Eating Championships* are held mid- to late-July at The Bottle Inn in the Dorset village of Marshwood.

Issued with two-foot-tall stinging nettle stalks, contestants have exactly one hour to strip and eat as many leaves as possible, after which time the bare stalks are measured and the winner declared. With the nettle stings causing tongues to swell and blacken and vomiting forbidden, most competitors either give up or find themselves disqualified.

World Pea-Throwing Championships

The first Sunday in October sees the annual *World Pea-Throwing Championships* held outside the Lewes Arms pub in the East Sussex town of Lewes. Contestants have three attempts at throwing a frozen pea down Castle Ditch Lane, the winner being the one whose pea travels the furthest. If a pea is lost down one of the lane's drains, the contestant is awarded an extra throw.

World Coal-Carrying Championships

If you enjoy humping make your way on an Easter Monday to the West Yorkshire village of Gawthorpe, where you will find the *World Coal-Carrying Championships*. Starting at the Royal Oak pub on Owl Lane, competitors must hump a 50-kg sack of coal 1108 yards and 3 inches to the finish line at the Maypole on the village green. The winner is crowned King (or Queen) of the Coil Humpers.

World Gurning Championships

If you happen to possess false teeth and a face that contorts like elasticated rubber, get yourself along to the small Cumbrian market town of Egremont for the *World Gurning Championships*.

With teeth removed or placed upside-down and head framed through a horse collar, rubber-faced contestants vie to pull a face best likened to chewing tobacco in a wind tunnel. Not overly complicated by judgement rules, the winner is the contestant who gains the most applause.

The World Gurning Championships are the highlight of the Egremont Crab Fair, held on the third Saturday in September. Dating back to 1267, the Crab Fair celebrates the time when the lord of the local manor wheeled a cart of crab apples through the then village as a goodwill gesture to the poor. According to folklore, the gurning competition originated from the faces the locals made when they bit into the sharp apples.

World's Biggest Liar

In November, the Bridge Inn in the Cumbrian village of Santon Bridge stages a contest to determine the world's biggest liar. The contest is held in memory of Will Ritson, proprietor in the 19th century of what is now the Wasdale Head Inn at the head of nearby Wastwater, England's deepest lake. Ritson gained a reputation for his 'tall stories', one infamous tale to visitors new to the area being that turnips grew so large in the Lake District, farmers would carve out the insides to provide sheds for their Herdwick sheep.

With each contestant allowed five minutes to recount their tall story, the *World's Biggest Liar* is open to all except politicians and lawyers, barred from entering as they are deemed too skilled.

World Custard Pie Championship

If you enjoy nothing better than a good pudding, around late May or early June the Kent village of Coxheath plays host to the *World Custard Pie Championship*.

Starting roughly three paces apart, each team of four hurls custard pies at the opposing team, with points awarded for accuracy, throwing technique and originality of costume.

World Snail Racing Championships

The month of July sees the Norfolk village of Congham come alive as it plays host to the *World Snail Racing Championships*. With no giant foreign snails allowed, common or garden English snails are plucked from their daily business of lurking under pots, placed in the inner braided circle of a damp tablecloth and, upon the command "Ready ... steady ... SLOW!" encouraged to race at top speed towards the outer circle finish line.

Limited by the table size, the course distance is thirteen inches, with a further four inches of table allowed for competitors to slow to a halt before crashing to the floor.

Chapter 7

David Peckham! David Peckham!

On 17 January 2009, at a Hertfordshire Senior Centenary Trophy quarterfinal football match between Hatfield Town and Hertford Heath, a parrot was sent off for imitating the referee's whistle. The parrot, a pet of a Hertford Heath fan, often attended the team's home games. And on that note, over to our sports desk for the full-time football roundup...

Uppies and Downies
With the Cumbrian seaside town of Workington sloping towards the harbour, residents on higher ground to the east, traditionally colliers, are known as Uppies, whilst

residents on lower ground to the west, traditionally seafarers, are known as Downies.

Each Good Friday, Easter Tuesday and the following Saturday on a piece of ground bordering the southern bank of the River Derwent known as the Cloffocks, the Uppies and Downies confront each other for three games of mass-participation football. The games have no rules, no time limit and no restriction on the number of players per side; the goals are one mile apart, one being a capstan at the harbour and the other the gates of Workington Hall, east of the town. Extra sporting interest has been added since the opening of a Tesco food store, approximately located if the 'pitch' were marked out with white lines, at what would be the centre circle.

The game ends when either the Uppies throw the ball over the capstan, or the Downies throw the ball over the gates.

Royal Shrovetide Football
Dating back to the 12th century, Shrovetide football was once popularly played throughout England on Shrove Tuesday, 47 days before Easter Sunday.

Although a fire in the 1890s destroyed records prior to 1667, the annual Shrovetide match played in the Derbyshire town of Ashbourne is thought to be the world's oldest, largest, longest and quite possibly maddest football match. Known locally as 'hugball', several thousand players (Up'ards by tradition born north of Henmore Brook, versus Down'ards born to the south) compete for two days with a hand-painted, cork-filled ball. Legend tells that the ball may have originally been a severed head, tossed into the onlooking crowd following a local execution.

Limited rules prohibit little more than murder, movement of the ball by vehicle and play after midnight. The goals are three miles apart and the game continues through the streets, residents' gardens and the river, with only the town's cemeteries, churchyards, memorial gardens, hospital and allotments off Watery Lane deemed out of bounds.

The game begins when the ball is tossed in the air – known locally as *turned up* – from a special plinth in what was Shaw Croft field, now a town centre car park.

Royal Assent was gained in 1928 when the Prince of Wales, later to become King Edward VIII, 'turned up'. For his troubles, he apparently received a bloody nose.

Contrary to the *football* name, the ball is rarely kicked, moving through the town in a *hug*: not unlike a traditional rugby scrum, only involving more players than can comfortably fit in an average town square.

Opposite to convention, a goal is scored when a team gets the ball to their own goal, the Up'ards' goal being Sturston Mill, the Down'ards' Clifton Mill. At least they were, except that both mills are long gone, quite possibly destroyed during a previous game.

To score, with the lack of a mill a player must hit the ball instead against the remaining millstone three times, with the team's scorer being a pre-selected local player to avoid an 'outsider' stealing the glory. Following a goal, the scorer is carried at shoulder height into the Boswell Bar of The Green Man Royal Hotel.

Of the limited rules, the 'no play after midnight' ruling is somewhat redundant as play kicks off both days at 2 p.m. and ends at 10 p.m., unless a goal is scored after 5 p.m., following which teams stop for the day and retire for liquid refreshment.

Hallaton Hare Pie Scramble and Bottle-Kicking
On Easter Monday, following a game of tug-of-war, a blessing at St Michael's Church and some almost-in-tune musical entertainment courtesy of the Hallaton Hare Pie Brass Band, a large hare pie is paraded through the streets of the Leicestershire village of Hallaton.

At the church gates the pie is chopped up and thrown to the gathered crowd, a scramble ensuing as the hungry throng fight to grab their morsel of food. At least, that may have been the case many generations ago before burgers and hotdogs were readily available from the church fundraising stall in the village square or the somewhat-out-of-place-among-the-thatched-cottages large American diner van topped with a six-metre-long wooden hotdog. Nowadays the crowd appear more concerned with not getting hare in their hair, the scraps of pie eagerly devoured by the less discerning local dog population.

Continuing to the village green, three small beer barrels, known locally as 'bottles', are decorated with ribbons. Two of the barrels contain beer but the third – the 'dummy', painted red, white and blue – is a relatively recent addition, introduced around 150 years ago to ensure that the ensuing game would have a winner.

Following the distribution of twelve small loaves and a passing hour or so for the locals to consume more beer from plastic glasses, the parade regroups to lead the crowd to the top of Hare Pie Hill, where the first of the 'bottles' is thrown into the air three times. Signalling the start of the game, several hundred players from the opposing village teams of Hallaton and Medbourne then attempt to 'kick' the bottle through the countryside between two streams.

Around one mile apart, the streams mark the opposing villages' boundaries and the winner is the first team to kick two bottles across their own village stream.

En route the teams must negotiate ditches, hedges, barbed wire and sheep droppings (together with the sheep responsible). The game has no time limit and rules are limited to no eye-gouging, strangling or use of weapons.

Legend tells that the centuries-old custom originated after two Hallaton women found themselves staring down the nostrils of a disgruntled bull.

Facing death, the women were saved after a hare distracted the irate animal.

Seeing this as an act of God, as a show of gratitude, the women donated a sum of money to the church. In return, the vicar was each Easter Monday to provide a hare pie along with twelve small loaves of bread and two barrels of beer, to feed the poor of the village. With the food somewhat sparing a fight would often ensue, and on one occasion villagers from neighbouring Medbourne, taking advantage of the distraction, stole the beer. So began the village rivalry.

Haxey Hood
Legend tells that in 1359 Lady Elizabeth de Mowbray, wife of wealthy landowner John de Mowbray, was riding over the hill between the North Lincolnshire villages of Haxey and Westwoodside, when she lost her silk riding hood to a gust of wind. Seeing what had happened,

thirteen local farm workers chased the hood all over the field – by all accounts, a comical scene.

The farm worker who caught the hood, too shy to return it to its owner, passed it to one of his fellow workers. Somewhat unkindly, Lady de Mowbray likened the worker who returned her hood to a Lord, whilst the worker who had caught the hood she dubbed a Fool. So amused was Lady de Mowbray by the whole affair that she donated land to the village on condition that each year the locals re-enacted the comical hood-chase. And so, to this day on

6th January (or 7th if the 6th is a Sunday) the people of Haxey and Westwoodside come together for Haxey Hood, likened to a game of mass-participation rugby football.

The day begins with a procession, making its way via the Duke William, The Loco and King's Arms pubs in Haxey and the Carpenter's Arms in Westwoodside to St Nicholas parish church. The Fool, a man dressed in rags with his face smeared with red ochre and soot, leads the procession. Atop the Fool's head sits a feathered hat decorated with flowers and various miscellaneous items. In one hand he grasps the Hood – a leather tube – and in the other hand a bran-filled sock attached to a whip.

As the procession advances the Fool has the right to kiss any woman en route.

Joining the procession is the Lord of the Hood, carrying his wand of office – a staff made from thirteen willow wands – along with the game's head referee, known as the Chief Boggin.

Both are dressed in hunting red with decorated top hats.

Alongside the Chief Boggin are a further eleven assistant Boggins, also dressed in red.

Upon arriving outside the church, the Fool stands on an old mounting block known as the Mowbray Stone and makes a welcoming speech. Whilst he speaks a fire is lit from behind using damp straw: an act known as 'Smoking the Fool'.

Lucky Fool, as prior to the 20th century a large fire would be lit below a tree. The Fool would then be hung from the tree and swung back and forth over the smouldering fire until gasping for breath, whereupon he would be dropped into the smoke and flames.

As the Fool finishes his speech the crowd chants along:

Hoose agen hoose,
Toon agen toon.
If a man meets a man, knoock 'im doon,
But doan't 'ot 'im.

The Fool then leads the crowd to Upperthorpe Hill for the game to begin. Following a warm-up event involving local children, the 'Sway Hood' (allegedly, originally a freshly slaughtered bullock's head) is thrown to the crowd. Quickly a huge scrum forms; with upward of 200 villagers, the scrum is known as the Sway, as it sways back and forth destroying everything from hedgerows to walls.

The game continues for several hours, as players attempt to manoeuvre the Hood to the door of one of the four local pubs. Once inside the pub the game ends and the Hood remains there on display until the following year.

Eton Wall Game
Located in the Berkshire village of Eton, Eton College is one of the most if not *the* most famous public school in the world. Its list of former pupils includes twenty British prime ministers. Quite a tally, and just enough for the two teams of ten players required for the *Eton Wall Game*. Dating back to at least 1766, the game, played on St Andrew's Day between a team of Collegers and Oppidans, has been described as 'one of the oldest, hardest and weirdest ball games in the world'.

The pitch, marked on one side by a slightly curved brick wall (hence the name), may be a mere five metres wide but what it lacks in width it makes up for in its 110-metre length.

The wall also provides ample seating for spectators.

With rules akin to a cross between rugby union and football, scrum-like 'bullys' are formed against the wall, having the effect as the bully scrapes up and down of a giant and painful exfoliation, removing the skin down one side of players immediately next to the wall.

The game has various moves, such as a *furk* where the ball is hooked backwards, and the formation of a *phalanx* – a diagonal tunnel from the bully for the ball to be passed along.

To score a goal, the ball must hit against a garden door at one end or a tree at the other, with a kicked goal scoring five points and a thrown goal nine. At least so they think. The last goal to be scored, at the time of writing, was in 1909.

Bodmin Hurl
In the Cornish town of Bodmin, the end of the ancient ceremony of Beating the Bounds marks the beginning of the *Bodmin Hurl*. The game begins when the Town Mayor throws a small sterling silver ball equal in size to a cricket ball into a pond known as the Salting Pool.

Having rushed to retrieve the ball, participants then attempt to get it to the finish line by the Turret Clock in Fore Street, travelling via Callywith Road, Castle Street,

Church Square and Honey Street. The player in possession of the ball when the mass scrum reaches the clock receives a £10 reward.

Although likened to mass-participation rugby football, with a set route and no teams the Bodmin Hurl may not appear too harsh a game; but be warned: legend tells that when local men defied the Sabbath by playing the game on a Sunday they instantly turned to stone. They now form three stone circles on Bodmin Moor, known as *The Hurlers*.

Beating the Bounds and in turn the Bodmin Hurl is held only once every five years, in years divisible by the number five; and rest assured whatever the date it will not be a Sunday.

Forever England

Chapter 8

Painting the Town Red

The expression 'drunk as a skunk' would have aptly described Henry Beresford, 3rd Marquess of Waterford, when he arrived in the Leicestershire town of Melton Mowbray in the early hours of 6 April 1837. Accompanied by his similarly inebriated friends, Beresford took the ladders, brushes and pots of paint left in readiness of redecorating the town's tollgates and proceeded to paint the town, including several police constables who attempted to intervene, red. It is from the Marquess's drunken activity that the English language gained the well-oiled expression, 'painting the town red'.

Speaking of raucous behaviour...

Berwick-upon-Tweed
Barely more than a trebuchet's slingshot south of the Scottish border, Berwick-upon-Tweed claims the dubious record for being the most embattled place in Europe, 'ownership' being exchanged between England and Scotland at least thirteen times. Still to this day, Berwick Rangers Football Club plays in the Scottish Football League (although to be fair, there may be other reasons for this).

As a warning to the Scottish, following his execution in 1305, William Wallace, their notorious leader in the Wars of Scottish Independence, was drawn and quartered and one of his arms put on display in the town.

Leatherhead
In the TV series *The Hitchhiker's Guide to the Galaxy* Arthur Dent's house, facing imminent demolition to make way for a planned bypass, was said to be in Leatherhead. The Surrey town fared little better in the H.

G. Wells book *The War of the Worlds*, withstanding the worst of a Martian attack.

A 2002 poll conducted by the Commission for Architecture and the Built Environment for BBC Radio 4 concluded that Leatherhead had the fifth worst high street in Britain. At the time Mole Valley Council, having recently paved the street and made it traffic free, were in the middle of spending a considerable amount of money installing a water feature in the town centre. Rather controversially, after months of disruption and problems with excavation work, the water feature didn't have – and never will have – any water.

Not to rest on its laurels, Leatherhead has since been shortlisted for the award of *The Most Boring Town in Britain*.

Keswick

The Cumbrian market town of Keswick gained its name from the old Celtic word for cheese. The town was the source of the world's first pencils, made from locally mined graphite. If at a loss at what to do on a rainy afternoon, the Cumberland Pencil Museum both explores the history of the writing implement and displays the world's largest colouring pencil.

Keswick was the first place in Great Britain where police used riot gear. The joke tells that it was a somewhat heavy-handed response to a man attempting to unfold a 1:3 scale Ordnance Survey map in the busy Tourist Information Office.

Stoke-on-Trent

In December 2013, Stoke-on-Trent became the first English city to be designated a disaster resilient zone by the United Nations. The UN's International Strategy for Disaster Resilience committee found the city fully prepared to deal with such events as flooding, aviation disaster and terrorism. Whether plans are in place in the event of the 'dormant' volcano two miles below Stoke unexpectedly erupting is another matter.

Dorking
There is a breed of chicken called the 'Dorking', which begs the question: What came first, the chicken or the Surrey town?

Letchworth Garden City

The UK's first 'gyratory traffic flow system' was built roundabout 1909 in the Hertfordshire town of Letchworth. When first opened, traffic could circulate the six-road intersection in whatever direction it chose. It was not until 1932 that KEEP LEFT signs were added.

Chapter 9

The Name's Pond ... Duck Pond

Ah, English village life – thatched cottages, cricket on the green, ducks on the pond, a set of medieval stocks where rotten vegetables were once thrown at anyone arrested for stealing little more than a potato, a hanging tree for the dispensing of passing highwaymen and a ducking stool for drowning suspected witches…

It's not all cake-baking and tea with the local vicar.

Blubberhouses

It may sound like underwater accommodation for whales, but the North Yorkshire village of Blubberhouses is thought to have acquired its name from *bluberhus*, the Anglo-Saxon word to describe houses built by a bubbling stream.

Once Brewed / Twice Brewed

The story tells that in 1751 the English army began work constructing a road across the north of England from Carlisle in the west to Newcastle in the east. The Military Road was to follow the line of Hadrian's Wall, the Roman-built divide between England and Scotland, making use of the stone from the redundant wall in its foundations. Manual labourers brought in to help with construction were housed at an inn midway between the two cities. Tired and thirsty from their long journey, the workers turned for refreshment to the inn's local ale.

Finding the ale rather weak, they requested that the proprietor brew the ale again, and from that day forth their place of rest became known as the Twice Brewed Inn.

Skip ahead a few years and in 1934 England's first Youth Hostel was built on Military Road, barely a stone's throw east of the Twice Brewed Inn. Officially opened by Lady Trevelyan, a staunch teetotaller, in referring to the Inn she reputedly declared, "Of course, there will be no alcohol served on these premises, so I hope the tea and coffee will only be brewed once." From that day forth, it became known as the Once Brewed Youth Hostel.

The Youth Hostel, together with the Twice Brewed Inn and the surrounding farms, now make up (according to the road signs as you enter) the village of *Twice Brewed* – incorrectly marked on maps as *Once Brewed* and known by some as *Once Brewed / Twice Brewed* – in what is now the Northumberland National Park.

Ugley
Far from being ugly, Ugley is a visually inoffensive Essex hamlet.

Pease Pottage
The West Sussex village of Pease Pottage is said to have earned its name from the passing trade of prisoners being transported between jails at Horsham and East Grinstead. The prisoners were fed pease pottage, a savoury pudding dish made from boiling peas until the coagulated mixture resembled green porridge.

Quaking Houses

The former County Durham coalmining village of Quaking Houses may have gained its name from its origin as a Quaker settlement. But then, an Ordnance Survey map printed in 1865 shows a Quaking House Farm to the north, with the Quaking Houses Branch Line railway passing close by carrying coal from the Quaker House Pit, close to the village.

Streets in the small village include Second Street, Third Street and Fourth Street, the former First Street now the site of a Community Hall.

Pity Me

Legend tells that the County Durham village of Pity Me was named in memory of St Cuthbert, who was said to have cried "Pity Me!" when monks accidentally dropped his coffin whilst passing through on their way to Durham.

Other theories suggest that the name may have derived from Petit Mere – French for a small lake – or

Pithead Mere, an area of boggy ground created by the wastewater pumped from the pithead of a local coalmine.

Somewhat on less boggy ground, the *Oxford Dictionary of British Place Names* suggests that Pity Me may have been a light-hearted name given in the 19th century to remote and exposed settlements where it was difficult to farm the land. A likely explanation, as there are several other albeit smaller Pity Me villages in the north of England, along with a Pityme in Cornwall.

Fence
The Lancashire village of Fence was named after a fenced enclosure erected to hold stag deer, hunted in nearby Pendle Forest.

Indian Queens

In the heart of Cornwall on the road from Goss Moor to Fraddon, there once stood The Queen's Head coaching inn. Around the 1780s, in commemoration of an overnight stay by an 'Indian Queen', the inn changed its name to The Indian Queen. The inn should have become The Portuguese Princess, as the 'Indian Queen' was a princess from Portugal on her way to London, having travelled by sea from her home country to the south coast port of Falmouth.

The alternative story tells that The Indian Queen changed its name in memory of a visit to the area in the early 17th century by Pocahontas, the famed daughter of American Indian chief Powhatan.

In commemoration of Queen Victoria being crowned Empress of India in 1877, The Indian Queen once again changed its name – this time to The Indian Queens.

Ignoring the truth of the Portuguese princess in favour of the more exciting story of Pocahontas, the inn's signboard depicted Victoria as Queen of India on one side and an American Indian on the other.

The Indian Queens was demolished in the 1960s, the inn's old signboard now in Truro Museum. Nevertheless, the name lives on in the village that grew up around the inn, the Cornish village of Indian Queens.

Wigwig
The Shropshire hamlet of Wigwig acquired its hairy name from an Anglo-Saxon settler named Wyga.

The Wallops
In the BBC television adaptations of Agatha Christie's *Miss Marple* novels, Dane Cottage in Five Bells Lane, Nether Wallop, features on screen as the exterior of Miss Marple's home. Much of the picturesque Hampshire village and surrounds can be seen throughout the 1980s series.

Nether Wallop is part of The Wallops. Sounding not unlike the effect a rollercoaster ride has on your stomach, The Wallops – Over Wallop, Middle Wallop and Nether Wallop – gained their name from *waella*, the old word for stream, and *hop* meaning a valley. The three villages follow the path of the Wallop Brook.

Twenty and Counter Drain

During construction of a railway line between the Lincolnshire towns of Bourne and Spalding in 1866, three intermediary stations were built to serve farms en route. Some distance from populated areas, the first station – *Twenty* – was named after a nearby milestone by the side of what is now the A151; the milestone signified that it was 20 miles to Colsterworth. The station has long gone, but the hamlet of Twenty remains.

Similarly, the station nearest to Spalding was named after a nearby drainage ditch: *Counter Drain Railway Station* has also long gone and, perhaps surprisingly, no hamlet developed.

Fryup

The North Yorkshire hamlet of Fryup is thought to have gained its full-English-breakfast name from Frigg-hop, Frigg being a Norse goddess and hop a small valley.

The Snorings

Referred to in the Domesday Book of 1086 as Snaringa, the sleepy Norfolk villages of Great Snoring and Little Snoring are thought to have developed in the 5th century when an Anglo-Saxon named Snear settled in the area.

Somewhat at odds with snoring, the Old English *snear* means swift, bright or alert. Also at odds, Little Snoring is bigger than Great Snoring.

Land of Nod
How the tiny East Riding of Yorkshire hamlet of Land of Nod acquired its sleepy name has been lost to time and, aside from quizzing the few farm animals that live there, there is very little chance of finding out.

Tiddleywink
The Wiltshire hamlet of Tiddleywink gained its name from rhyming slang for 'a quick drink', one of the cottages being a watering hole for passing cattle herders.

Mardale Green
Don't hold your breath in expectation of a refreshing pint at the Dun Bull Hotel, a centuries-old inn in the Cumbrian village of Mardale Green. Once popular with Lake District ramblers and climbers, the pub along with the remainder of the village was submerged under water in 1935 following the construction of Haweswater

Reservoir. Parts of the village are visible when the water level is low.

Chapter 10

Oh! I Do Like to Be Beside the Seaside

Donkeys, deckchairs, windbreaks and knotted hanky hats, nuclear power stations, sewage ... oh! I do like to be beside the seaside...

Bournemouth Sewage Works
The beaches around the south coast resort of Bournemouth are some of the cleanest in England, thanks in no small part to Wessex Water. If it is a little too windy to get the deckchairs out and bask in the glorious summer sunshine, the local water authority offers the occasional vintage bus guided tours of Bournemouth Sewage Works.

Given that 500,000 litres of local sewage pass through the treatment works pipes each day, perhaps a windy day is not the best time to pay a visit.

Sellafield

The nuclear reprocessing plant on the west Cumbrian coast at Sellafield is currently storing around 120 tonnes of enriched plutonium, the biggest stockpile of the deadliest manufactured substance on Earth.

Drigg

On the west Cumbrian coast bordering the Lake District National Park, just a short jog south of Sellafield, the village of Drigg boasts sandy beaches and dunes and is both a local nature reserve and a designated Site of Special Scientific Interest. The village is also home to a storage facility for low-level toxic waste from the country's nuclear power stations, hospitals, medical companies, oil industry and Ministry of Defence sites. In February 2009, the facility's new owners LLW Repository Ltd, upon discovering that disposal records were akin to a jigsaw with a few missing pieces, placed the following advert in the local Whitehaven News:

'We need your help. Did you work at Sellafield in the 1960s, 1970s or 1980s? Were you by any chance in the job of disposing of radioactive material? If so, the owners of Britain's nuclear waste dump would very much like to hear from you: they want you to tell them what you dumped – and where you put it.'

One would hope, not amongst the sand dunes.

Dungeness

Dry, windy and lacking vegetation, the south coast headland of Dungeness was England's only official desert until in August 2015 a spoilsport at the Met Office dismissed this as an urban myth.

Dungeness is home to two nuclear power stations. Final decommissioning and closure of Dungeness A, deactivated in 2006, is scheduled for 2111. Meanwhile, an expanse of water known to anglers as 'the boil' boasts rich sea life courtesy of the 100 million litres of hot water (and the odd litre-or-two of sewage) pumped each hour into the sea from Dungeness B via two outfall pipes.

Nodding Donkey, Kimmeridge Bay
Nothing to do with an agreeable member of the horse family, the 'nodding donkey' above Dorset's Kimmeridge Bay is England's oldest working oil pump. In continuous operation since 1961, the pump extracts oil from 350 metres below the cliff.

Although its original output of 350 barrels a day has steadily declined to 65, total oilage (were there such a word) to date is roughly 3 million barrels, enough oil to three-quarter fill the world's largest super tanker.

Hartlepool

It was the early 19th century, a time of the Napoleonic Wars, and the people of Britain were petrified of an invasion led by the French Navy. In the County Durham fishing town of Hartlepool men kept a vigilant watch out to sea, until one stormy night a French warship was blown onto the rocks, smashing to pieces and sinking below the turbulent waves. All souls were lost. All that is, except – legend tells – the ship's mascot, a monkey that for inexplicable reasons had been dressed in a French military uniform.

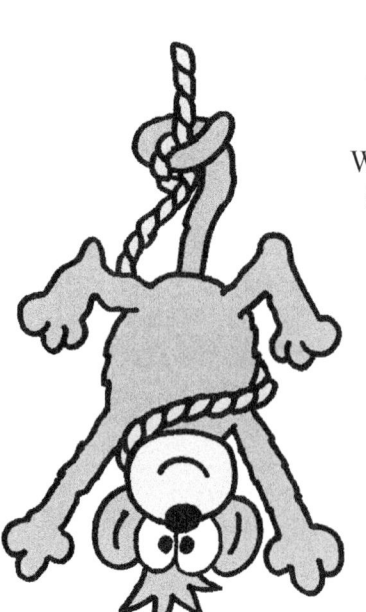

With travel not being what it is today the locals of the town, having never seen either a monkey or a French person, presumed them the same. The hapless creature, obviously a French spy, was brought before the court, found guilty and hanged.

For many generations, the people of Hartlepool were derided for their simple mistake, until in 1999 Hartlepool United Football Club adopted H'Angus the Monkey as its mascot. A popular character, in 2002 H'Angus stood in the town's mayoral election with a manifesto of free bananas for schoolchildren. He won a landslide victory and at the time of writing has since served a further two terms in office.

Southport Beach
Legendary racehorse, Red Rum, three-time winner of the Aintree Grand National, used to train on Southport beach.

Saltburn Funicular Cliff Railway
Opened in 1884, the funicular railway at the North Yorkshire seaside resort of Saltburn-by-the-Sea is the oldest water-balance cliff-lift still in operation in England. Carrying up to ten passengers, downward movement is created by adding water to the car at the top of the cliff until its weight exceeds that of the car at the beach below. As the top car lowers the bottom car automatically rises.

Newquay Beach
Following its premiere at a Paris fashion show in 1946, later that year Maisie Dunn became the first woman to wear a bikini on an English beach – the beach at Newquay.

Studland Bay
Enid Blyton and her second husband Kenneth used to holiday each summer on the south coast, staying at the Grand Hotel in Swanage. Toy Town, home to the

characters in her popular *Noddy* books, is thought based on the nearby village of Studland, P.C. Plod inspired by Christopher Rhone the local police officer.

The Bay at Studland is famous for its naturist beach. Five go naked in Studland.

Chapter 11

Nudge, Nudge, Wink, Wink

From Lickham Bottom to Titty Ho, the shires of England are awash with place names that would bring colour to the cheeks of a parish vicar.

Say no more...

Long Lover Lane
A quiet spot overlooking Halifax, the *Long* of Long Lover Lane refers to the lane's length, not the stamina of its late-night visitors.

Lickham Bottom
Part of Lickham Common, Lickham Bottom is a valley between Hackpen Hill and Castle Hill, southwest of the Devon village of Hemyock.

Pant

It may sound like a remnant of men's underwear following a severe boil wash, but the Shropshire village of Pant claims its name from the Welsh word for hollow or valley.

The village lies close to the Welsh border, below the disused copper mines of the Llanymynech Rocks Nature Reserve.

Shitterton

In a 2012 survey by an ancestral search company, Shitterton was voted the UK's most embarrassing place name. To add insult to toilet humour, the Dorset hamlet of thatched cottages is recorded in the Domesday Book of 1086 as Scatera, or Scetra, meaning a little town set on a stream that runs from a sewer.

With Shitterton's name sign constantly stolen by collectors of toilet-humour artefacts, in 2010 residents clubbed together to buy a replacement chiselled from a one and a half tonne block of Purbeck stone set into concrete.

Titty Ho
The Northamptonshire town of Raunds is home to a street with the unusual name of Titty Ho. Although the origin of the name has been lost to time, one theory

suggests that 'Ho' could be short for house, and that the house may have once been popular with birds.

Wetwang
The East Riding of Yorkshire village of Wetwang may have earned its name from the Viking expression for a field where legal courts held session.

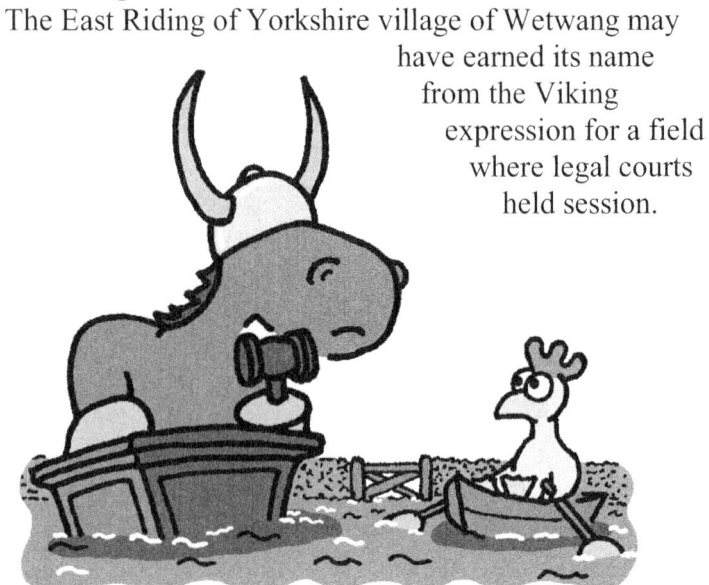

But then the name could have come from 'wet field', given that the village is just west of the 'dry field' town of Driffield.

Crotch Crescent
With crotch being a fork in a tree, Crotch Crescent, in the Marston suburb of Oxford, may have once been a forest.

Aunt Mary's Bottom
Providing a rich habitat for plants and wildlife, Aunt Mary's Bottom is a designated Site of Special Scientific Interest on the northern slope of Rampisham Hill, north of the Dorset town of Dorchester.

Chapter 12

Follywood

A mock church tower, is never dour
Hooray for Follywood...

Mad Jack's Sugar Loaf

Legend tells that in the 1820s, Member of Parliament and renowned philanthropist John 'Mad Jack' Fuller bet the vicar of St Giles Church in the East Sussex village of Dallington that he could see the church spire from the garden of his house, three miles away in Brightling. Upon returning home, he realised that there was a hill in the way and so, to win the bet, he had a stone folly built midway, the steeple-like cone resembling a church spire above the distant trees. A little under eleven metres tall, the stone cone sits all alone in a field off the B2096 Battle to Heathfield road.

Known as Mad Jack's Sugar Loaf, the cone gained its sweet name from the dome-shaped 'loaf' that refined sugar was sold in during the 19th century. Not to put a good folly to waste, with exterior windows and a ladder between its two floors, the stone cone became home to a Simon Crouch and his wife, their daughter Mabel being born there in 1879.

The Pyramid
John Fuller lived in what is now Brightling Park, next to the Church of St Thomas-à-Becket in the East Sussex village of Brightling. He earned the nickname 'Mad Jack' as he was a prolific folly builder. Perhaps his greatest folly was his own mausoleum, a nearly eight-metre-high stone pyramid erected in the churchyard in 1811, 23 years before his death.

The story once told that Fuller was laid to rest in the pyramid in full evening dress, seated at a table upon which was placed a fine bottle of Port and a roast chicken meal, with the floor covered with broken glass to keep the devil at bay.

Renovation work on the Pyramid in 1982 proved the story untrue. Fuller was buried, conventionally, in the soil underneath.

Rushton Triangular Lodge
Dating back to 1597, Rushton Triangular Lodge sits in the former grounds of the Tresham Estate, a short stroll from the Northamptonshire village of Rushton. Built with alternating bands of dark and light sandstone, the lodge is not only, as you might guess, triangular: each of the three walls is 33 feet long, with three triangular windows below three gargoyles and three triangular gables. A three-sided obelisk, in the centre of which stands a triangular chimney decorated with three-lobed 'trefoil' leaf patterns, crowns each gable. Upon entrance, a Biblical quotation from St John's Gospel reads *Tres Testimonium Dant*. The inscription loosely translates as 'there are three that bear witness'.

A devout catholic, towards the latter part of the 16th century Sir Thomas Tresham found himself imprisoned on several occasions for refusing to attend Anglican Church services. Emerging from prison in 1593, he designed the Triangular Lodge as a visual sign of his faith, the number three being a symbol of the Trinity, with God as the Father, the Son and the Holy Ghost.

The House in the Clouds
Having inherited his parents' Suffolk coast estate in 1908, wealthy Scottish barrister and playwright Glencairn Stuart Ogilvie purchased the fishing hamlet of Thorpe to the north, intending to transform it into Thorpeness, an exclusive playground village for the wealthy, with holiday cottages, a country club and an artificial boating lake. By 1923, Ogilvie's vision was all

but complete excepting that the new and essential 21-metre-tall water tower was proving something of an eyesore. Not content to let things be, he had the steel-framed tower disguised as a five-storey cottage, with fake windows on the level of the water tank, a pitched roof above and living accommodation below.

At first calling it the Gazebo, Ogilvie later renamed his creation *The House in the Clouds* following a poem describing the tower by his friend, a local writer of children's stories known only as Mrs Malcolm Mason.

In 1943, whilst a German V1 rocket passed overhead a wayward shell from a Bofors anti-aircraft gun pierced the southeast corner of the water tank, creating more than a slight issue with damp. At the time two women, both answering to the name of Miss Humphrey, slept on below unaware that they would find themselves somewhat short of water for their morning cup of tea.

With Thorpeness connected to the mains water supply, in 1979 the tower's water tank was removed and the fake windows replaced, making a somewhat tall five-bed holiday cottage overlooking Thorpeness Golf Course and the Suffolk coast.

White Nancy

Here's to the mountain of Nancy
That's built upon Ingersley Hill
Here's good health, wealth and fancy
And give Dodd another gill!

Nearly six metres tall and resembling a gnome's hat topped with a small ball, White Nancy stands proudly atop Kerridge Hill, overlooking the Cheshire town of Bollington. The folly is thought to have been built around 1817 by a Colonel Gaskell, either as a summerhouse or to commemorate Britain's victory at the Battle of Waterloo; Gaskell lived below the hill at Ingersley Hall.

The story tells that the local builder in charge of construction was named Dodd, and he christened the folly White Nancy after the white horse that hauled the cart with the building materials up the steep hill.

Once with a door and small window set into bare bricks, White Nancy appears to have since been coated either in icing sugar or an extremely thick layer of bird droppings, as the surface is now smooth and white and the door and window lost inside.

Jack the Treacle Eater
Marking the eastern boundary of the Barwick Park Estate, close to the Somerset village of Barwick, is a five-metre-high arch built from jagged stone blocks. Above the arch, a stone staircase leads to a wooden door set within a small round tower. Atop the tower's pointed cone roof is a lead statue of the Roman god Mercury; the statue appears to be running. The story goes that Jack, servant to the Messiter family, owners of the Barwick House and Estate, lived in the tower. Upon the family's request Jack would run the 110 miles to London to deliver their mail, with nothing but a jar of treacle to sustain him.

Honouring the Messiter family's molasses-eating servant, the folly – built around 1775 – is known as Jack the Treacle Eater.

The Headington Shark

Feeling, in his own words, 'a sense of impotence and anger and desperation' following the nuclear disaster at Chernobyl in 1986, Bill Heine decided that the best way to express his feelings was to erect a fibreglass shark on the roof of his house at 2 New High Street, in the Oxford suburb of Headington. Despite initial guffawing from the local council, the eight-metre tail remains to this day.

The Needle's Eye
"Again, I tell you, it is easier for a camel to go through the eye of a needle than for a rich man to enter the kingdom of God."

(The Gospel According to Matthew; Chapter 19: Verse 24)

Legend tells that, somewhat worse for wear following a night of heavy drinking, Earl Fitzwilliam, the 2nd Marquis of Rockingham, bet that he could steer his horse and carriage through the eye of a needle.

The following morning, the sober Earl – at the time one of the wealthiest men in England – began work on the design of a fourteen-metre-high 'needle' topped with a decorative urn. Contained within the needle would be a Gothic arch, just a little wider than his horse and carriage.

Built around 1746, the Needle's Eye once straddled a single-track private road from the Earl's South Yorkshire country manor of Wentworth Woodhouse to the Lion Lodges to the north. Although the road has since returned to grass the folly still exists, albeit slightly pockmarked from musket-balls, a further story telling that it was once used for the execution of prisoners by firing squad.

Chapter 13

Foreign Correspondence

When Dame Vera Lynn sang of bluebirds over the White Cliffs of Dover, they were at the time still part of England...

St Margaret's Bay
Part of the village of St Margaret's-at-Cliffe, St Margaret's Bay sits below the famous White Cliffs of Dover. As the nearest point to the French mainland and blocked by the cliffs from receiving mobile phone signals from home networks, St Margaret's Bay is a little telecommunications enclave of France.

Mobile phone users regularly receive 'Welcome to France' messages, with the village said to be popular with French tourists eager to take advantage of cheap phone calls on their home network.

Lumbfoot

Following a dispute with the neighbouring village of Stanbury, in 1989 the West Yorkshire hamlet of Lumbfoot declared its independence from the UK. Immediately pronouncing Lhasa, the capital of Tibet, as its twin-town, residents erected a road barrier and, appearing to acquire the status of a French principality, assigned two former outside toilets as a *douane* – a French customs and excise agency – and a *gendarmerie* – a French police station.

Given the name Lumbfoot, inhabitants of the hamlet may well have taken offence at continually being mistaken for an unpleasant complaint involving a lower limb. La réponse, je ne sais pas.

Runnymede

In 1965, two years after his assassination, a memorial to US President John F. Kennedy was erected in the meadows at Runnymede, close to where 750 years earlier King John had signed *Magna Carta*, The Great

Charter of Liberties of England. The acre of land surrounding the memorial is part of America, given to the United States by the people of Britain.

The Sahara
If you park your car nowhere near a beach and return to find it coated in a layer of yellowy-red dust, chances are it is sand from the Sahara carried in the atmosphere from North Africa following a particularly severe sandstorm.

If you later report this to the international police organization Interpol do remember that *Sahara* in Hebrew translates as *desert*, so it is the Sahara, not the Sahara Desert.

The Principality of Sealand
As part of anti-aircraft defence measures during the Second World War, seven Maunsell Sea Forts were floated out to sea and lowered into shallow waters off the east coast of England.

One of the island fortresses, HM Fort Roughs, was sunk on to Rough Sands, a sandbar six miles off the coast of Suffolk. With British territorial waters at the time extending only three miles from shore, HM Fort Roughs rested in international waters.

Decommissioned in the late 1950s, the Maunsell Sea Forts fell into disrepair, becoming home in the mid-sixties to pirate radio stations, with the occupation of

Fort Roughs a disputed battle between Radio Caroline and the owner of Radio Essex, a former British Army major by the name of Paddy Roy Bates. Bates, having been forced to close Radio Essex following his conviction for illegally broadcasting from a sea fort within British coastal waters, was looking to claim 'land' outside of British authority.

Despite Radio Caroline having stationed two men on the abandoned fort to claim occupancy rights, on Christmas Eve 1966 Bates sent four men to seize the platform.

With a new parliamentary act soon to come into force banning pirate radio broadcasts from former sea forts, on 14 September 1967 Bates declared Fort Roughs an independent sovereign state.

The British Royal Navy, sent to investigate, found itself fired upon for entering the State's 'territorial waters' and Bates and his son were arrested.

Tried on weapons charges, the Judge dismissed the case, declaring that as Fort Roughs lay beyond British territorial waters a court held no authority over its international affairs.

Assuming this as official recognition of independence, in 1975 Bates established a national flag and anthem, issuing local currency, stamps and passports and, with the writing of a State Constitution, declaring the former sea fort the *Principality of Sealand*. He also declared himself His Royal Highness Prince Roy.

Later passing the Principalities' affairs to his son Michael, His Royal Highness Prince Roy himself passed on in October 2012.

Although remaining unrecognised by any established sovereign state, the Principality of Sealand – an iron platform the size of two tennis courts sitting atop twin steel-reinforced concrete towers – claims to be the world's smallest nation.

Chapter 14

Flotsam and Jetsam

The Angel of the North
Four double-decker buses in height, with the wingspan of a Jumbo Jet and seen by 90,000 motorists every day, the Angel of the North is England's biggest and the world's most commonly viewed piece of public art. Towering above both the A1 and A167 from Low Fell, south of the Tyne and Weir town of Gateshead, Antony Gormley's 200-tonne winged-human is affectionately known as the Gateshead Flasher.

A1101
Barely rising above sea level, the A1101, running 53 miles from Bury St Edmunds in Suffolk to Long Sutton in Lincolnshire, is the lowest road in England.

Willy Lott's House, Suffolk
As the name suggests, Willy Lott's House was once home to tenant farmer Willy Lott. Built in the 16th century, the house – on the banks of the River Stour in the Suffolk hamlet of Flatford – features in John Constable's famed painting, *The Hay Wain*.

When Constable finished The Hay Wain in 1821 his father owned nearby Flatford Mill. The mill features in several of his other paintings.

Ham and Sandwich
The Kent village of Worth was once home to a signpost pointing to both the village of Ham and the nearby town of Sandwich, but following numerous thefts the local council no longer bother replacing it.

There is however (at the time of writing) a similar sign at the southern end of West Street, between Ham and Finglesham.

Stott Hall Farm, M62
When the trans-Pennine M62 motorway was under construction in the 1970s the planned route was to take it through Stott Hall Farm, close to the West Yorkshire moorland village of Scammonden. The 18th-century farm was spared the bulldozers when it was found to be sitting on unstable land that was liable to subsidence. Instead, the carriageways were rerouted parting just enough to pass either side of the farm buildings.

With nearly 300,000 vehicles speeding past its windows every day, the isolated farm is known locally as 'the little house on the prairie'.

The House That Moved, Exeter
With a new inner by-pass planned for the city of Exeter, 16 Edmund Street, a timber-framed merchant's house thought to date back to the mid-15th century, was in the way. As the bulldozers moved in for the scheduled demolition, Exeter City Council bowed to local pressure

and granted the house protected status, listing it for its architectural and historic significance. The problem was it was still in the way.

The solution was simple – strip the house down to its timber frame, encase it within a protective cradle, place it on wheels and move it 70 metres up the hill to the bottom of West Street. And so, after several weeks of preparation, on Saturday 9 Sept 1961 the 21-tonne building began its five-day journey to its new location.

Sadly, following restoration, barring a few timbers little remains of the original structure, and *The House That Moved* sits in the shadow of a busy inner by-pass, a reminder of a time when progressive-planning meant bulldozing the city's historic past.

Northumberlandia
Constructed on farmland near to the Northumbrian town of Cramlington, Northumberlandia is described as 'a human landform sculpture of a reclining female figure'. Four hundred metres long with breasts thirty-four metres in height, the Naked Lady of the North – known to locals as Slag Alice – was landscaped from 1.5 million tonnes of spoil from the adjacent Shotton opencast coal mine.

St Andrew's Church Clock, Wootton Rivers
With dials on three of the four sides of the square tower of St Andrew's Church, in the Wiltshire village of Wootton Rivers, the dial facing away from the village

has instead of traditional Roman numerals, the letters GLORY BE TO GOD.

The tower also houses a very odd clock, built to commemorate the coronation of King George V in 1911 by local farmhand and watch repairer, Jack Spratt. Spratt constructed the clock's mechanism from bicycle parts, including chain cogs and a bell…

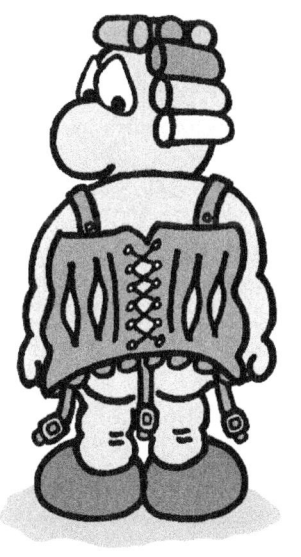

…along with piano keys, stays from a corset, metal from old saucepans and various other pieces of scrap.

Sourcing parts from local barns, sheds and outside toilets, a broom handle provided the pendulum, and the chimes – linked to the peel of five bells within the tower – appear to have come from the workings of a wind-up music box.

With Jack Spratt's time on Earth up the clock fell into disrepair. Remaining silent for several years, it was later restored for the Queen's Silver Jubilee in 1977 with the aid of copper tubing, an old brass hinge and a float arm removed from a toilet cistern.

To mark the Millennium, electrical winding gear was installed and an extra bell added, making Jack Spratt's original music box mechanism somewhat out of time. Not only that, to mark every quarter-hour it would play a different and randomly out-of-time tune.

Since then the broom handle pendulum has finally fallen off and – until someone searches their outside toilet for some new parts – time once again stands still in the Wiltshire village of Wootton Rivers.

Not one to rest on his melodious laurels, the story tells that Jack Spratt also invented a musical toilet.

When sat upon the toilet would play a tune, and the heavier the person relieving themselves the faster the tune would play. It didn't catch on.

Tiggywinkles
Named after the prickly star of Beatrix Potter's *The Tale of Mrs. Tiggy-Winkle*, Tiggywinkles was at the time of its foundation in 1983 the world's first hedgehog hospital. Originally caring for hedgehogs that had fallen victim to such things as cars, cats and lawnmowers, the hospital, in the Buckinghamshire village of Haddenham, now opens its doors to everything from badgers to buzzards, many of the ten thousand wild animals treated each year too sick or injured to return to their natural habitat, living out their life at the hospital.

And they all lived happily ever after...

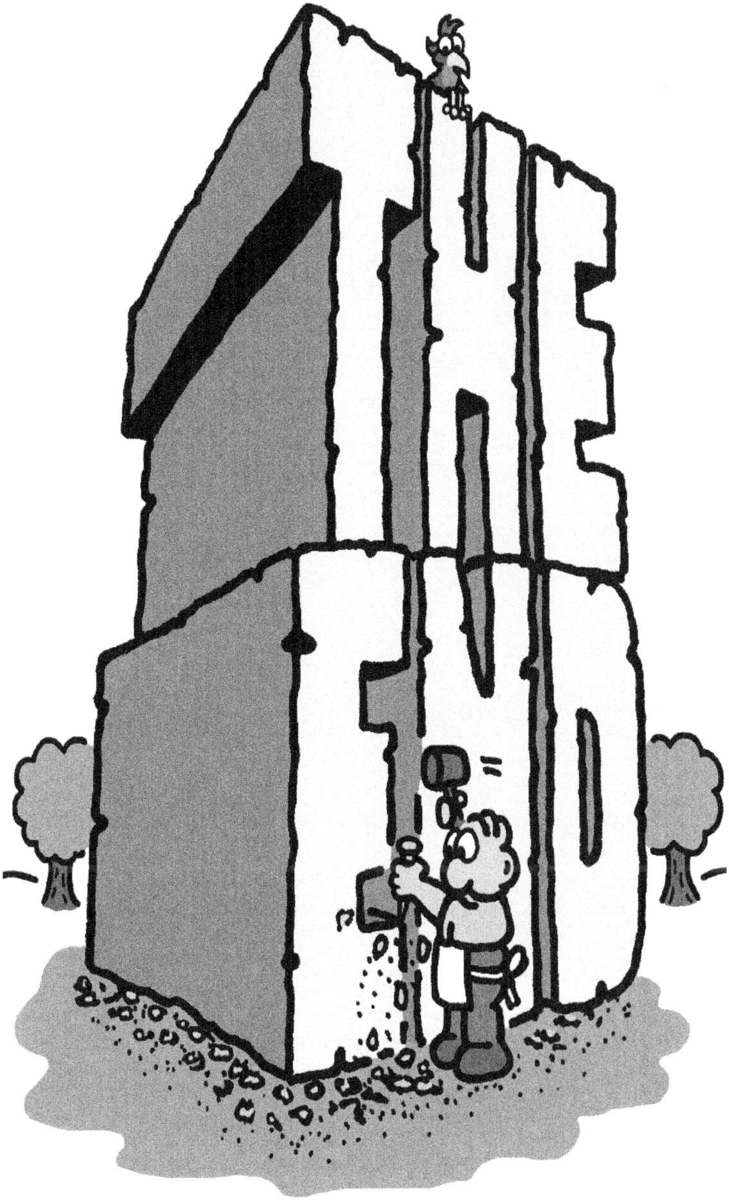
THE END